STEVE JOBS

LEGENDS AND LEGACIES

THE BIOGRAPHY OF STEVE JOBS

Published by
Rupa Publications India Pvt. Ltd 2024
7/16, Ansari Road, Daryaganj
New Delhi 110002

Sales centres:
Bengaluru Chennai
Hyderabad Jaipur Kathmandu
Kolkata Mumbai Prayagraj

Copyright © Rupa Publications India Pvt. Ltd 2024

The views and opinions expressed in this book are the author's own and the facts are as reported by him which have been verified to the extent possible, and the publishers are not in any way liable for the same.

All rights reserved.
No part of this publication may be reproduced, transmitted, or stored in a retrieval system, in any form or by any means, electronic, mechanical, photocopying, recording or otherwise, without the prior permission of the publisher.

P-ISBN: 978-93-6156-975-3
E-ISBN: 978-93-6156-532-8

First impression 2024

10 9 8 7 6 5 4 3 2 1

Printed in India

This book is sold subject to the condition that it shall not, by way of trade or otherwise, be lent, resold, hired out, or otherwise circulated, without the publisher's prior consent, in any form of binding or cover other than that in which it is published.

Contents

Introduction	7
Early Life (1955-1972)	9
Formative Years (1973-1976)	13
Founding Apple (1976-1980)	17
The Rise and Fall (1981-1985)	22
NeXT and Pixar (1985-1996)	28
Return to Apple (1997-2001)	35
Innovation and Dominance (2001-2011)	45
Personal Life	55
Final Years and Legacy (2011-Present)	62
Lessons From Steve Jobs's Life	75
Conclusion	79

Introduction

Imagine a world without smartphones, tablets, or sleek, easy-to-use computers. It's hard to picture, isn't it? Much of the technology we rely on today exists because of one man: Steve Jobs. His innovative ideas and creative vision changed the way we live, work, and play, making him one of the most influential figures in modern history.

Steve Jobs was born on February 24, 1955, in San Francisco, California. From a young age, he was curious and full of ideas. This curiosity led him to explore electronics and gadgets, sparking a lifelong passion for technology. Little did anyone know that this passion would eventually lead to the creation of one of the most successful companies in the world: Apple Inc.

In 1976, Steve Jobs co-founded Apple Inc. with his friend Steve Wozniak in his parents' garage. They started by building and selling a computer kit called the Apple I. This was just the beginning. Under Jobs's leadership, Apple introduced a series of groundbreaking products that revolutionized technology. The Macintosh computer, released in 1984, was one of the first personal computers to feature a graphical user interface, making it much easier for people to use.

But it was the launch of the iPhone in 2007 that truly changed the world. The iPhone combined a phone, a music player, and an internet communicator into one device, and it set the standard for smartphones. Today, millions of people around the world use iPhones to stay connected, work, and have fun. Following the iPhone, Apple introduced the iPad, which transformed how we read books, watch movies, and browse the internet.

Jobs's influence wasn't limited to Apple. In 1986, he bought a small computer graphics company called Pixar from filmmaker George Lucas. Under Jobs's leadership, Pixar created some of the most beloved animated films of all time, including Toy Story, Finding Nemo, and The Incredibles. These films not only entertained millions but also pushed the boundaries of animation and storytelling.

Throughout his life, Steve Jobs was known for his passion, creativity, and determination. He had a unique ability to see the potential in new ideas and was never afraid to take risks. Jobs believed in the power of innovation and always strived for excellence. His famous motto, "Stay hungry, stay foolish," encouraged people to keep exploring and never be afraid of failure.

Steve Jobs faced many challenges along the way. In 1985, he was forced to leave Apple after a power struggle within the company. But he didn't give up. Instead, he started a new company called NeXT, which developed powerful computers for businesses and schools. In a twist of fate, Apple later bought NeXT, bringing Jobs back to the company he had started. This reunion marked the beginning of Apple's most successful period, with the launch of iconic products like the iMac, iPod, iPhone, and iPad.

Jobs's story is a testament to the power of perseverance and the belief that anything is possible if you have the courage to follow your dreams. He left behind a legacy of innovation and creativity that continues to inspire people around the world.

1

Early Life (1955-1972)

Birth and Adoption

Steve Jobs's story begins on February 24, 1955, when he was born in San Francisco, California. His birth parents, Joanne Schieble and Abdulfattah Jandali, were young and not ready to raise a child, so they made the difficult decision to place him for adoption. Steve was adopted by Paul and Clara Jobs, a loving couple who couldn't have children of their own. Paul was a machinist and Clara was an accountant, and they raised Steve in a nurturing home in the heart of Silicon Valley, a place that would later become synonymous with technological innovation.

Childhood in California

Growing up in California, Steve was a curious and energetic child. His father introduced him to the world of electronics and mechanics, teaching him how to take apart and rebuild gadgets. Paul Jobs had a workbench in the garage, and it was here that young Steve developed a fascination for understanding how things worked. This early exposure sparked Steve's passion for

Stephen Jobs

technology and gave him hands-on experience that would be invaluable later in life.

Early Interest in Electronics and Gadgets

Steve spent hours in the family garage, tinkering with old radios, televisions, and other electronics. He even tried to build a rudimentary computer by wiring together spare parts. This passion for understanding the inner workings of devices laid the foundation for his future innovations.

When Steve Jobs was just 12 years old, he managed to land an internship at HP by cold-calling the company's CEO, Bill Hewlett. He found Hewlett's number in the local phone directory and decided to give it a shot. Jobs introduced himself and asked for spare parts to build a frequency counter. To his surprise, Hewlett not only gave him the spare parts, but also offered him a summer job at Hewlett Packard, working on the assembly line. This experience was a dream come true for the young Jobs.

High School Years and Friendships

During his high school years at Homestead High in Cupertino, California, Steve met a fellow student named Steve

Steve Wozniak

Wozniak. Wozniak, known as "Woz," shared Steve's love for electronics, and together, they formed a lasting friendship. The two Steves bonded over their enthusiasm for technology and would spend countless hours working on projects together.

> **Fun Fact**
> Jobs and Wozniak's blue boxes were so successful that they once used them to prank call the Vatican, pretending to be Henry Kissinger and asking to speak to the Pope.

One of their early collaborations was creating and selling "blue boxes," devices that allowed people to make free long-distance phone calls. This small venture was not only profitable but also gave them a taste of what it was like to create and sell a product, foreshadowing their future success with Apple.

Brief Stint at Reed College

After graduating from high school in 1972, Steve enrolled at Reed College in Portland, Oregon. However, he found the college environment restrictive and dropped out after just one semester. Despite leaving school, Steve continued to attend classes that interested him, like calligraphy. This seemingly random choice would later influence the elegant design of Apple's typefaces and user interfaces.

Influences and Mentors During His Formative Years

During his formative years, Steve Jobs was influenced by many people and experiences. One of his early mentors was Robert Friedland, a charismatic entrepreneur whom Steve met at Reed College. Friedland introduced Steve to Eastern spirituality and meditation, which would become a significant part of his life and philosophy.

Steve's travels to India in search of spiritual enlightenment also had a profound impact on him. He spent seven months in India, exploring the country, seeking guidance from spiritual leaders,

> **Fun Fact**
> Steve's father, Paul Jobs, once gave him a workbench and various tools, fostering Steve's early interest in electronics by showing him how to build and fix things.

and immersing himself in the culture. This journey taught him about simplicity, focus, and the importance of intuition—principles that would later shape Apple's product designs.

Steve Jobs's early life was marked by a relentless curiosity and a willingness to take risks. His experiences in California, his friendship with Steve Wozniak, his brief time at Reed College, and his travels and mentors all contributed to shaping the innovative thinker he would become. These early influences set the stage for Steve's incredible journey in the tech industry, where he would go on to change the world with his visionary ideas and groundbreaking products. His story is a testament to the power of perseverance, creativity, and the belief that if you think differently and work hard, you can achieve extraordinary things.

2

Formative Years (1973-1976)

Dropout and Spiritual Journey in India

After making the bold decision to drop out of Reed College in 1972, Steve Jobs embarked on a transformative journey that would shape his future endeavors. Feeling the pull of exploration and seeking deeper meaning, Jobs set off for India in 1974. He immersed himself in the rich tapestry of Indian culture, spending seven enlightening months traversing the country, meditating in ashrams, and engaging in soul-searching conversations with spiritual leaders. This sojourn not only broadened his horizons but also instilled in him a profound sense of mindfulness and purpose that would influence his approach to life and work.

Early Work Experiences

Upon returning from his spiritual quest, Steve Jobs was eager to apply his newfound insights to the world of technology. He landed a job at Atari, a pioneering video game company, where he worked as a technician. Immersed in the fast-paced world of arcade gaming, Jobs honed his skills in hardware design and software development, gaining invaluable hands-on experience that would prove instrumental in his future endeavors.

Atari Inc. logo (1973)

At Atari, Jobs demonstrated his trademark ingenuity by devising creative solutions to technical challenges and pushing the boundaries of what was possible in the realm of computer engineering. His innovative spirit and relentless pursuit of excellence earned him a reputation as a visionary thinker and a formidable force in the burgeoning field of technology.

During his time at Atari, Steve Jobs was tasked with designing a circuit board for the game Breakout. He recruited his friend, Steve Wozniak, to help him complete the project, offering him half of the $700 bonus he received for finishing it within a tight deadline. Wozniak managed to simplify the design significantly, completing the task in just four days and earning them both the bonus.

Forming a Partnership with Wozniak

While at Atari, Steve Jobs reconnected with his high school friend and kindred spirit, Steve Wozniak. Wozniak had been tinkering with building his own computer, the Apple I, as a hobby. Recognizing the potential of Wozniak's invention, Jobs proposed forming a partnership to bring the computer to market. In 1976, the two Steves founded Apple Computer Company in Jobs's parents' garage, with the audacious vision of democratizing personal computing and empowering individuals to unleash their creative potential.

Learning from Early Failures and Successes

The early years of Apple were a rollercoaster ride of triumphs and setbacks, successes and failures. The Apple I, while a modest success, served as a springboard for the groundbreaking Apple II, released in 1977. The Apple II revolutionized the personal computing industry, boasting innovative features such as a built-in keyboard, color graphics, and expandable memory. Its user-friendly design and intuitive interface made it a game-changer, capturing the imagination of consumers and catapulting Apple to the forefront of the tech revolution.

Apple II (1977) model in Apple Museum, Prague

Despite their early successes, Apple faced formidable challenges, including internal conflicts, production delays, and fierce competition from rival companies. In 1985, amidst mounting tensions and power struggles, Steve Jobs was ousted from Apple.

Undeterred, he channeled his entrepreneurial spirit into founding NeXT, a computer company focused on innovation and excellence. He also acquired Pixar Animation Studios, which would later become a powerhouse in the world of animated filmmaking.

Steve Jobs's formative years were defined by a relentless pursuit of innovation, a willingness to embrace failure as a stepping stone to success, and an unwavering commitment to pushing the boundaries of what was possible. His spiritual journey in India, early work experiences at Atari, partnership with Wozniak, and the ups and downs of founding Apple all played pivotal roles in shaping his visionary leadership and indelible legacy in the world of technology and beyond.

3

Founding Apple (1976-1980)

The Creation of Apple in Jobs's Garage

In the bustling suburb of Los Altos, California, amidst the serenity of a suburban neighborhood, a revolution was brewing. In 1976, Steve Jobs and Steve Wozniak, two visionary young men with a shared passion for technology, embarked on a journey that would forever alter the course of history. With little more than determination, ingenuity, and a garage as their headquarters, they founded Apple Computer Company. This humble beginning, born in the Jobs family garage, marked the inception of what would become one of the most influential and iconic companies in the world.

The iconic Apple logo, featuring a stylized apple with a bite taken out of it, was designed by Ronald Wayne, the third

Steve Wozniak

co-founder of Apple. Wayne sold his share of the company for just $800, missing out on billions in potential wealth.

The Development and Launch of the Apple I and Apple II

With their fledgling company taking shape, Jobs and Wozniak set out to create their first product: the Apple I. Designed by Wozniak and assembled by hand in the Jobs family garage, the Apple I was a bare-bones computer kit that represented a monumental leap forward in personal computing. Despite its simplicity, the Apple I captured the imagination of early tech enthusiasts, laying the groundwork for Apple's future success.

Apple I

Building on the momentum of the Apple I, Jobs and Wozniak unveiled their next innovation: the Apple II. Released in 1977, the Apple II was a game-changer in the world of personal computing. With its built-in keyboard, color graphics, and expandable memory, the Apple II set a new standard for innovation and usability. Its intuitive interface and user-friendly design made it a hit with consumers, catapulting Apple to the forefront of the tech industry.

The original Apple II prototype, known as the "Apple-1 ACI Cassette Interface," was sold by Wozniak at the 1977 Homebrew Computer Club for $40. Today, it is considered one of the most valuable pieces of computer history, fetching millions at auction.

Apple II

Early Success and Growth of Apple Inc.

Buoyed by the success of the Apple II, Apple Inc. experienced rapid growth and expansion. The company's innovative products and visionary leadership captured the imagination of consumers and industry experts alike, propelling Apple to the pinnacle of the tech industry. Sales of the Apple II soared, and Apple quickly became a household name, synonymous with cutting-edge technology and creative innovation.

Under Jobs's guidance, Apple cultivated a culture of innovation, creativity, and excellence that set it apart from its competitors. Jobs instilled in his employees a sense of purpose and passion for

> **Fun Fact**
> Steve Jobs personally called customers who wrote letters of praise or complaint about Apple products, demonstrating his commitment to customer satisfaction and his hands-on approach to leadership.

pushing the boundaries of what was possible, inspiring them to think differently and strive for greatness. This culture of innovation would become a hallmark of Apple's identity and a key driver of its success in the years to come.

The Apple II was used by NASA for scientific research and data analysis during the development of the Space Shuttle program, highlighting its versatility and reliability.

Jobs's Vision and Its Influence on the Company's Culture and Products

Steve Jobs's vision for Apple extended far beyond the realm of technology. He believed in creating products that not only met the needs of consumers but also inspired and delighted them. Jobs's relentless pursuit of perfection and his unwavering commitment to excellence permeated every aspect of Apple's culture and products, from design and engineering to marketing and customer experience.

Jobs's emphasis on simplicity, elegance, and intuitive design became the guiding principles behind Apple's iconic products. He famously declared, "Design is not just what it looks like and feels like. Design is how it works." This focus on user experience and attention to detail set Apple apart from its competitors and cemented its reputation as an industry leader in design and innovation.

First Major Milestones and Achievements

During its formative years, Apple achieved several major milestones and accomplishments that solidified its position as a pioneering force in the tech industry. In 1977, the company went public, generating significant capital and catapulting Jobs and Wozniak to newfound wealth and fame. The success of the Apple II propelled Apple to become the fastest-growing company in American business history at the time.

Apple III

In 1980, Apple further expanded its product lineup with the introduction of the Apple III, a business-oriented computer aimed at corporate customers. While the Apple III faced challenges and setbacks, it demonstrated Apple's commitment to innovation and its ambition to conquer new markets.

The Apple III suffered from design flaws that led to overheating and reliability issues, earning it the nickname "The Cube." Despite its shortcomings, the Apple III paved the way for future advancements in business computing and solidified Apple's reputation as a leader in the industry.

Steve Jobs's vision, leadership, and relentless pursuit of excellence were instrumental in shaping Apple's early success and laying the groundwork for its future achievements. His innovative spirit, passion for perfection, and unwavering commitment to pushing the boundaries of what was possible would continue to define Apple's culture and products for decades to come.

4

The Rise and Fall (1981-1985)

The Development of the Macintosh

After the success of the Apple II, Steve Jobs was determined to create a computer that would be accessible to everyone. His vision was for a machine that was not only powerful but also user-friendly, making computing a delightful experience for the masses. This vision culminated in the development of the Macintosh.

Jobs assembled a team of brilliant engineers and designers, often referred to as "pirates," who worked tirelessly on the project. The team included notable figures such as JefRaskin, who initially conceived the idea, and Bill Atkinson, who developed the revolutionary graphical user interface (GUI). The Macintosh project was characterized by innovation and secrecy, as the team worked in a separate building, often late into the night, to realize Jobs's vision.

> **Fun Fact**
> The Macintosh was named after JefRaskin'sfavorite type of apple, the McIntosh. To avoid a conflict with the audio equipment manufacturer McIntosh Laboratory, the name was deliberately misspelled.

Developing the Macintosh was no easy task. The team faced numerous technical challenges, such as fitting all the components into a compact case and making the software easy to use. Jobs was known for his perfectionism, often demanding changes and improvements that pushed the team to their limits. This drive for excellence, while stressful, resulted in a product that was ahead of its time. The original Macintosh team signed their names on the inside of the Macintosh's case. This was Jobs's way of recognizing their hard work and dedication, though customers never saw these signatures.

The 1984 Launch of the Macintosh and Its Initial Impact

On January 24, 1984, Steve Jobs unveiled the Macintosh to the world during a now-iconic presentation at Apple's annual shareholders meeting. The event was marked by the debut of the famous "1984" Super Bowl commercial, directed by Ridley Scott, which portrayed the Macintosh as a revolutionary force against the conformity represented by IBM.

Macintosh 128k

The launch was a spectacular success, generating immense public interest and excitement. The Macintosh's GUI, featuring icons, windows, and a mouse, was unlike anything the general public had seen before. It promised to make computing more intuitive and accessible, opening up new possibilities for both personal and professional use.

> **Fun Fact**
> The "1984" commercial aired only once during the Super Bowl, but it had a lasting impact, becoming one of the most famous advertisements in history.

Despite the initial excitement, the Macintosh faced challenges. It was priced at $2,495, which was quite expensive for most consumers. Additionally, it had limited software available at launch, which restricted its usefulness. While it was a technological marvel, its high cost and limited applications meant that sales were slower than anticipated. The Macintosh team placed an easter egg in the original Macintosh. If you opened a certain file, you would see a picture of the development team along with the message, "Here's to the crazy ones."

Internal Conflicts and Power Struggles at Apple

Despite the initial success of the Macintosh, trouble was brewing within Apple. The high cost of the Macintosh and its limited software library posed significant challenges. Additionally, Jobs's management style, characterized by high demands and intense scrutiny, led to friction within the company. His mercurial temperament created a polarized atmosphere, with some employees deeply loyal to him and others feeling alienated.

> **Fun Fact**
> Jobs once asked Sculley, "Do you want to sell sugar water for the rest of your life, or do you want to come with me and change the world?" This line famously persuaded Sculley to join Apple.

Internal conflicts reached a peak as Jobs clashed with Apple's then-CEO, John Sculley, whom Jobs had recruited from PepsiCo. Sculley and the board were concerned about the direction of the company and the financial viability of the Macintosh. These tensions culminated in a power struggle that would significantly alter the course of Jobs's career.

John Sculley

The tension between Jobs and Sculley was not just about business decisions but also about leadership styles and visions for the company's future. Jobs's aggressive and often abrasive approach contrasted sharply with Sculley's more traditional, structured management style. This clash eventually led to a dramatic showdown in Apple's boardroom. Jobs and Sculley initially bonded over their mutual love for marketing and design, but their relationship soured as they disagreed over the future direction of the company.

Jobs's Departure from Apple in 1985

In 1985, the power struggle between Steve Jobs and John Sculley came to a head. The board of directors sided with Sculley, leading to Jobs being stripped of his managerial duties. Feeling marginalized and without control, Jobs made the difficult decision to resign from Apple, the company he had co-founded and nurtured from its inception.

Jobs's departure marked a significant turning point in his life and career. It was a humbling experience, forcing him to reflect on his leadership style and the decisions that led to his ouster.

> **Fun Fact**
> After leaving Apple, Jobs sold all but one of his shares in the company as a symbolic gesture of his discontent. The single share allowed him to continue receiving the company's annual report and attend shareholder meetings.

However, Jobs did not let this setback define him. Instead, he channeled his energy into new ventures, determined to prove his critics wrong.

During his time away from Apple, Jobs founded NeXT, a computer company focused on creating high-end workstations for the education and business markets. Though NeXT computers were not commercially successful, the company's technology would later play a crucial role in Apple's resurgence when Jobs returned. The operating system developed by NeXT eventually became the foundation for Mac OS X, the operating system used in modern Macintosh computers.

Reflections on Early Lessons Learned

The period from 1981 to 1985 was a time of intense highs and lows for Steve Jobs. The development and launch of the Macintosh showcased his visionary brilliance and ability to inspire innovation. However, the internal conflicts and his eventual departure highlighted the challenges of leadership and the importance of balancing visionary ideas with practical execution.

From these experiences, Jobs learned valuable lessons about humility, resilience, and the importance of teamwork. He realized that even the most innovative ideas require careful management and strategic planning to succeed. These lessons would prove invaluable as he embarked on new ventures and eventually returned to Apple, wiser and more determined than ever.

During his time away from Apple, Jobs also acquired Pixar Animation Studios from George Lucas. Under Jobs's leadership, Pixar produced the first fully computer-animated feature film, "Toy Story," which became a massive hit and solidified Jobs's reputation as a visionary leader beyond the tech industry. Jobs initially bought Pixar for $10 million, but the company went on to become a powerhouse in animation, eventually being acquired by Disney for $7.4 billion, making Jobs Disney's largest individual shareholder at the time.

> **Fun Fact**
>
> Jobs once reflected on his departure from Apple by saying, "Getting fired from Apple was the best thing that could have ever happened to me. It freed me to enter one of the most creative periods of my life."

Steve Jobs's rise and fall at Apple during this period is a testament to his unyielding passion for innovation and his ability to learn from adversity. His experiences during these formative years would shape his future endeavors, ultimately leading to his triumphant return to Apple and the creation of some of the most iconic products in technology history.

5

NeXT and Pixar (1985-1996)

NeXT logo

Founding NeXT Inc.

After his departure from Apple in 1985, Steve Jobs was eager to start fresh and continue his quest to innovate. He founded NeXT Inc. with a vision to create advanced workstations aimed primarily at the higher education and business markets. Jobs invested $7 million of his own money to get the company off the ground and brought together a team of talented engineers and designers who shared his passion for cutting-edge technology.

Jobs's vision for NeXT was to build the ultimate computing machine that combined powerful hardware with a sophisticated software environment. The first product, the NeXT Computer, was unveiled in 1988. It was a sleek, black magnesium cube that housed advanced technology, including a 25 MHz Motorola 68030 processor, 8 MB of RAM (expandable to 64 MB), and a built-in Ethernet port.

NeXT Cubes and NeXTstation

Challenges and Innovations at NeXT

The NeXT Computer was a marvel of engineering and design, but it faced several significant challenges. Priced at $6,500, it was far too expensive for the average consumer or even many educational institutions. Additionally, while the hardware was impressive, the software ecosystem needed to be more developed, limiting the machine's usefulness.

Despite these challenges, NeXT made several important contributions to the field of computing. One of its most significant innovations was the NeXTSTEP operating system. NeXTSTEP was an advanced operating system that introduced several features that

> **Fun Fact**
>
> Tim Berners-Lee, the inventor of the World Wide Web, developed the first web browser and web server on a NeXT computer at CERN in 1990, marking a significant milestone in the history of the Internet.

would become industry standards, including a graphical user interface with a dock, the use of Display PostScript for on-screen graphics, and object-oriented programming frameworks that made software development more efficient. The programming environment of NeXTSTEP laid the groundwork for what would become macOS and iOS, significantly influencing modern software development practices.

NeXT also pioneered the use of magneto-optical drives for data storage, which, while not widely adopted, demonstrated Jobs's willingness to experiment with new technologies. Additionally, the company introduced the concept of rapid application development with Interface Builder, a tool that allowed developers to design graphical user interfaces visually.

> **Fun Fact**
> "Toy Story" was the first animated film to receive a Special Achievement Academy Award, recognizing its groundbreaking achievement in animation.

Acquisition of The Graphics Group, Later Renamed Pixar

In 1986, Steve Jobs acquired The Graphics Group, a division of Lucasfilm's computer graphics department, for $10 million. Renamed Pixar, the company initially focused on creating high-end computer graphics hardware and software. However, the hardware business did not take off as expected, leading Pixar to shift its focus to creating animated short films to showcase its technology.

Jobs recognized the creative potential of Pixar's talented team, including Ed Catmull and John Lasseter. Lasseter, a former Disney animator, had a vision for using computer animation to tell compelling stories. With Jobs's support, Pixar produced several short films, including "Luxo Jr." and "Tin Toy," which showcased the company's capabilities and won critical acclaim."Luxo Jr.," Pixar's first short film, introduced the iconic Pixar lamp, which became the company's mascot. The film was nominated for an Academy Award for Best Animated Short Film in 1986.

Pixar Studios

The Success of Pixar and Its Impact on the Film Industry

Pixar's big breakthrough came in 1995 with the release of "Toy Story," the first fully computer-animated feature film. The film was a massive success, both critically and commercially, grossing over $350 million worldwide. "Toy Story" was praised for its innovative animation, engaging story, and memorable characters, and it became an instant classic.

Following the success of "Toy Story," Pixar released a string of hit films, including "A Bug's Life" (1998), "Toy Story 2" (1999), and "Monsters, Inc." (2001). Each film pushed the boundaries of animation and storytelling, further solidifying Pixar's reputation for excellence.

> **Fun Fact**
>
> "Toy Story" was the first animated film to receive a Special Achievement Academy Award, recognizing its groundbreaking achievement in animation.

Pixar's films have had a profound impact on popular culture and the film industry. Movies like "Finding Nemo" (2003), "The Incredibles" (2004), "Ratatouille" (2007), and "WALL-E" (2008) not only entertained audiences of all ages but also conveyed important messages about family, identity, and environmental responsibility."Finding Nemo" was so influential that it led to a temporary decline in wild clownfish populations due to increased demand from pet owners, a phenomenon known as the "Finding Nemo Effect."

The Merger of Pixar with Disney

In 2006, Pixar merged with The Walt Disney Company in a deal worth $7.4 billion. This merger not only brought significant financial benefits but also allowed Pixar to maintain its creative independence while leveraging Disney's extensive distribution network and marketing resources. Steve Jobs became Disney's largest individual shareholder and joined its board of directors.

The merger proved to be highly successful, leading to a new era of blockbuster films, including "Up" (2009), "Toy Story 3" (2010), and "Inside Out" (2015). Pixar continued to innovate, producing films that pushed the boundaries of animation technology and storytelling.

Fun Fact

"Toy Story 3" was the first animated film to gross over $1 billion worldwide, demonstrating the enduring popularity of Pixar's storytelling.

The Role of Creativity and Vision in Driving Success

Throughout his time at NeXT and Pixar, Steve Jobs demonstrated the importance of creativity and vision in driving success. At NeXT,

Walt Disney Pictures Logo

he pushed the boundaries of computer technology, creating innovations that would later influence the entire tech industry. At Pixar, he nurtured a culture of creativity and excellence, enabling the studio to produce some of the most beloved animated films of all time.

Jobs's ability to envision the future and his relentless pursuit of perfection were key factors in his success. He believed in the power of great ideas and the importance of bringing together talented individuals to achieve extraordinary results. His experiences at NeXT and Pixar not only shaped his approach to business but also reinforced his belief in the transformative power of technology and storytelling. Steve Jobs was awarded a Special Achievement Academy Award in 1996 for his significant and technical contributions to the computer industry, highlighting his impact beyond traditional business success.

During his time at Pixar, Jobs learned valuable lessons about managing creative teams and the importance of fostering an environment where innovation could thrive. He understood that great ideas often come from collaboration and that providing the right tools and support could lead to groundbreaking achievements.

Steve Jobs's journey from NeXT to Pixar was marked by challenges, innovation, and remarkable achievements. His unwavering commitment to excellence and his ability to inspire creativity in others left an indelible mark on both the technology and entertainment industries. These experiences would eventually lead to his triumphant return to Apple, where he would continue to change the world with his visionary leadership. The NeXT acquisition by Apple in 1996 brought Jobs back to the company he co-founded, marking the beginning of a new era of

> **Fun Fact**
> Jobs insisted that the new Pixar Animation Studios headquarters be designed to encourage random encounters and collaboration among employees, believing that creativity often sparked from these informal interactions.

innovation at Apple. The technology and talent from NeXT played a crucial role in developing macOS, which revitalized Apple's product line and set the stage for future successes like the iMac, iPod, iPhone, and iPad.

Steve Jobs's ability to blend technology with art and his relentless pursuit of excellence made him a unique and influential figure. His time at NeXT and Pixar demonstrated his resilience, creativity, and visionary thinking, qualities that would define his legacy and continue to inspire future generations.

6

Return to Apple (1997-2001)

The Acquisition of NeXT by Apple

In the mid-1990s, Apple faced a dire situation. The company was struggling with declining market share, financial instability, and a lack of innovation. Seeking a solution, Apple decided to acquire NeXT Inc. for $429 million in December 1996. This acquisition not only brought Steve Jobs back to the company he had co-founded but also introduced NeXT's advanced technology into Apple's ecosystem. The NeXTSTEP operating system, renowned for its robust architecture and user-friendly interface, became the foundation for what would eventually evolve into macOS, the operating system that powers modern Mac computers.

When Steve Jobs returned to Apple, his role was initially as an advisor. However, his influence quickly grew as he began to reshape the company's direction and strategy. Jobs's official title during this period was "iCEO," a playful reference to his interim status and his focus on revitalizing Apple's identity. His return marked the beginning of a remarkable transformation for the company.

Jobs's Return to Apple and the Revitalization of the Company

Steve Jobs rejoined Apple in 1997 as interim CEO, a role that eventually became permanent. His return marked the beginning of a remarkable transformation for the company. One of his first actions was to streamline Apple's product line, which had become cluttered with numerous models and variations. Jobs introduced a simplified product matrix, focusing on just four main categories: consumer desktops, consumer laptops, professional desktops, and professional laptops. This move helped the company focus its resources and regain its footing in the market.

In addition to streamlining the product lineup, Jobs also tackled Apple's financial woes. He secured a $150 million investment from Microsoft in 1997, which provided much-needed capital and helped stabilize Apple's finances. This strategic partnership also included commitments to continue developing Microsoft Office for Mac, ensuring that Apple users would have access to essential productivity software.

> **Fun Fact**
> The "Think Different" campaign featured famous figures such as Albert Einstein, Martin Luther King Jr., and Mahatma Gandhi, positioning Apple as a brand that championed innovation and creativity.

Jobs's impact on Apple was immediate and profound. He made tough decisions, such as discontinuing outdated products and refocusing the company's efforts on innovation and quality. His ability to envision the future and his relentless pursuit of excellence began to steer Apple back on course.

Introduction of the iMac and the Resurgence of Apple's Brand

In 1998, Apple unveiled the iMac, a revolutionary computer that departed from the traditional beige boxes of the era. Designed by JonyIve, the iMac featured a colorful, translucent case and an all-in-one design that integrated the monitor and CPU into a single

iMac G3 Strawberry

unit. The iMac was not only visually striking but also easy to set up and use, making it appealing to consumers and educators alike.

The iMac's design and marketing campaign emphasized simplicity and creativity, playing a crucial role in revitalizing Apple's brand. It quickly became a best-seller, helping to stabilize Apple's finances and restore consumer confidence in the company. The "i" in iMac stood for "internet," reflecting the computer's ease of use in connecting to the rapidly growing internet. The iMac's success marked the beginning of Apple's resurgence as a major player in the tech industry. The iMac's colorful design was inspired by a gumdrop, and its translucent case allowed users to see the inner workings of their computer, a radical departure from the opaque, boxy designs of the time.

Key Hires at Apple

Steve Jobs knew that turning Apple around required more than just new products; it needed a cultural overhaul. He recruited top talent, bringing in executives like Tim Cook, who became Chief Operating Officer and later succeeded Jobs as CEO. Cook's expertise in supply chain management helped streamline Apple's operations, making the company more efficient and cost-effective. Another notable hire was Jonathan Ive, whose innovative design concepts would become integral to Apple's identity.

Jobs fostered a culture of innovation and excellence at Apple. He encouraged a collaborative environment where designers, engineers, and marketers worked closely together to create products that were not only functional but also aesthetically pleasing. This emphasis on design and user experience became a hallmark of Apple's brand. Jobs was known for his "top 100" meetings, where he would gather Apple's top employees to brainstorm and plan the company's future, ensuring that the best ideas were given priority. Jobs was known for his meticulous attention to detail and his insistence on perfection. He famously redesigned the layout of Apple's cafeteria to encourage more spontaneous interactions among employees, fostering a collaborative atmosphere.

Johnny Ive

Turning Around a Struggling Company

When Jobs returned to Apple, the company was on the brink of

manufacturing processes, reduce costs, and improve efficiency. This operational overhaul was critical in ensuring that Apple could meet the growing demand for its products without compromising

Tim Cook with Mike Bloomberg

on quality.

Jobs also brought in JonyIve, whose innovative design concepts became integral to Apple's identity. Ive's design philosophy, which emphasized simplicity, functionality, and beauty, aligned perfectly with Jobs's vision for Apple. Together, they worked on products that not only performed well but also looked stunning and were easy to use.

Jobs fostered a collaborative environment at Apple, encouraging designers, engineers, and marketers to work closely together. He believed that the best ideas came from the intersection of different disciplines and that fostering a culture of creativity and excellence was essential for innovation. Jobs was known for his "top 100" meetings, where he would gather Apple's top employees to brainstorm and plan the company's future, ensuring that the best ideas were given priority. Jobs's meticulous attention to detail extended to every aspect of Apple's operations, including the design of the company's cafeteria. He believed that a well-designed environment could inspire creativity and foster collaboration among employees.

Turning Around a Struggling Company

When Jobs returned to Apple, the company was on the brink of bankruptcy. Through a combination of strategic decisions and innovative products, he managed to turn the company around. One key decision was to cut down the vast array of products Apple was offering and focus on a few core products. This simplification helped Apple allocate resources more effectively and ensured higher quality in its offerings.

Jobs also focused on improving Apple's retail presence. In 2001, Apple opened its first retail stores, designed to provide customers with a u5nique and immersive shopping experience. These stores allowed Apple to control its brand image and provide better customer service, contributing to increased sales and customer loyalty. The first Apple Store opened in Tysons Corner, Virginia, on May 19, 2001. The concept was so successful that it eventually led to hundreds of stores worldwide. The design of Apple Stores was revolutionary, featuring a minimalist aesthetic with large glass windows and open floor plans. Jobs was heavily involved in the design process, even down to the type of wood used for the tables.

Strategic Decisions that Led to Apple's Comeback

Several strategic decisions made by Jobs during this period were instrumental in Apple's resurgence. One of the most critical was the development of Mac OS X, a new operating system based on NeXTSTEP. Mac OS X provided a stable and user-friendly platform that attracted both consumers and professional users, helping to differentiate Apple from its competitors. This operating system laid the foundation for the seamless integration of software and hardware, a hallmark of Apple's products.

Jobs also placed a strong emphasis on industrial design and

the user experience. By focusing on these areas, Apple was able to create products that stood out not only for their performance but also for their aesthetic appeal and ease of use. This focus on design and usability was evident in the development of the iBook and the Power Mac G4 Cube, both of which showcased innovative design elements.

Another critical decision was the introduction of the iPod in 2001. The iPod

ipod Classic 6th gen

revolutionized the music industry by offering a portable, easy-to-use device that could store thousands of songs. Its success not only boosted Apple's revenues but also paved the way for future innovations like the iPhone and iPad. The idea for the iPod originated from a meeting between Jobs and Apple engineer Jon Rubinstein, who discovered a small, high-capacity hard drive that could be used to store music files. This discovery led to the creation of a device that transformed how people listened to music. The first generation of the iPod used a tiny 1.8-inch hard drive, which was a breakthrough in storage technology at the time. Jobs's insistence on a minimalist design meant that the device had only five buttons, which made it incredibly simple to use.

Jobs's strategic vision extended beyond product development to include partnerships and acquisitions. For instance, the investment from Microsoft in 1997 was not just a financial lifeline; it also ensured continued support for Microsoft Office on Mac, which was crucial for many professional users. This partnership helped stabilize Apple's customer base and provided a bridge to the company's future successes.

Steve Jobs also focused on improving Apple's marketing and branding efforts. The "Think Different" campaign launched in 1997 became an iconic representation of Apple's philosophy. The

Think Different campaign (1984 with First Macintosh)

campaign celebrated the idea of challenging the status quo and thinking creatively, which resonated deeply with both consumers and the tech community.

Steve Jobs's return to Apple marked a new era of success and innovation for the company. His strategic decisions, coupled with his ability to inspire and lead, revitalized Apple and set the stage for some of the most iconic products in technology history. This period laid the groundwork for the extraordinary achievements that would follow, solidifying Jobs's legacy as one of the most influential figures in the tech industry.

7

Innovation and Dominance (2001-2011)

Launch of the iPod and Transformation of the Music Industry

In October 2001, Apple introduced the iPod, a sleek, portable music player that would forever change how people listened to music. The iPod could store up to 1,000 songs on its tiny 1.8-inch hard drive, and its simple, intuitive interface made it easy to use. Steve Jobs envisioned a device that would make it effortless for people to carry their entire music libraries in their pockets, revolutionizing personal music consumption. This product was an instant hit, not just because of its capabilities but also because of its stylish design, which set it apart from other MP3 players on the market.

The iPod's influence extended beyond just the hardware. In 2003, Apple launched the iTunes Store, which allowed users to purchase and download music legally and easily. This move transformed the music industry by providing a viable alternative to illegal file-sharing and changing how music was distributed and consumed. The combination of the iPod and iTunes Store created a powerful ecosystem that solidified Apple's dominance in digital music.

ipod mini 1G

The iPod line expanded over the years, introducing new models like the iPod Mini, iPod Nano, and iPod Shuffle, each designed to cater to different consumer needs. The iPod Touch, introduced in 2007, added a multi-touch interface and access to the App Store, making it more like a smartphone without the phone capabilities. The name "iPod" was inspired by the iconic line "Open the pod bay doors, HAL" from the movie "2001: A Space Odyssey." Jobs wanted a name that conveyed a futuristic and innovative image, reflecting the device's cutting-edge technology.

> **Fun Fact**
> The circular scroll wheel, a defining feature of the iPod, was not invented by Apple. It was based on a prototype created by a company called Synaptics.

Development and Release of the iPhone, and Its Revolutionary Impact

In January 2007, Steve Jobs stood on stage at the Macworld Conference & Expo and introduced the iPhone, a revolutionary device that combined a mobile phone, an iPod, and an internet communicator into one sleek package. The iPhone featured a large, multi-touch display, a virtual keyboard, and an elegant design that set it apart from the bulky and complex smartphones of the time. Jobs famously described the iPhone as three devices in one: a phone, an iPod, and an internet communicator.

The iPhone's impact was immediate and profound. It redefined the smartphone market, leading to a new era of mobile computing. The introduction of the App Store in 2008 allowed developers to create applications for the iPhone, creating a thriving ecosystem that further enhanced the device's functionality. The iPhone's success not only transformed Apple into one of the most valuable companies in the world but also influenced countless industries, from telecommunications to entertainment.

The first iPhone was revolutionary for its use of a capacitive touchscreen, which responded to the touch of human fingers rather than a stylus. This technology allowed for more precise and responsive touch inputs, enabling features like multi-touch gestures, which became a hallmark of Apple's devices. The iPhone also introduced a user-friendly operating system, iOS, which provided a seamless and intuitive user experience.

First iPhone

When the first iPhone was launched, it was initially met with skepticism from some industry experts who doubted its potential. However, it went on to sell over 6 million units in its first year, proving the critics wrong. The first-generation iPhone did not have an App Store. Apps were pre-installed on the device, and it wasn't until a year later that the App Store launched, allowing third-party developers to create apps for the iPhone. Apple was not the first to develop a touchscreen smartphone; however, it was the first to make it user-friendly and desirable to a broad audience, changing the perception and usage of mobile phones.

The Creation of the iPad and Its Influence on Computing

In January 2010, Apple unveiled the iPad, a tablet computer that aimed to fill the gap between smartphones and laptops. The iPad featured a large, multi-touch display, a lightweight design, and a user-friendly interface, making it ideal for browsing the web, reading e-books, watching videos, and using apps. The iPad's versatility and ease of use made it popular among a wide range of users, from students to professionals.

The iPad's influence on computing was significant. It introduced a new category of devices that combined the portability of smartphones with the functionality of laptops. The iPad's success spurred the development of numerous apps tailored for its larger screen, further enhancing its capabilities. It also had a major impact on industries such as education, healthcare, and business, where it was adopted for various applications.

The iPad's introduction also marked a shift in how people consumed digital content. With its large screen and powerful processing capabilities, the iPad became a popular device for streaming video, reading digital books and magazines, and playing games. The App Store, which had already been a success on the iPhone, provided a vast array of apps specifically designed for the iPad, ranging from productivity tools to creative applications. The idea for the iPad predates the iPhone. Jobs initially envisioned a tablet device but shifted focus to the smartphone first, believing it had greater immediate potential. The success of the iPhone paved the way for the iPad's development and launch. The original iPad was

iPad WiFi 1st Gen

designed without a physical keyboard, a move that was initially controversial but ultimately set the standard for modern tablets. During its development, the iPad was referred to internally as the "K48."

Jobs's Leadership Style and Vision

Steve Jobs was known for his visionary leadership and his ability to inspire and motivate those around him. His leadership style was characterized by a relentless pursuit of excellence, attention to detail, and a focus on innovation. Jobs had a unique ability to anticipate market trends and understand what consumers wanted, often before they even knew it themselves.

Jobs was also known for his demanding nature. He pushed his teams to achieve the highest standards, believing that great products required great effort. His hands-on approach and insistence on perfection sometimes led to intense work environments, but it also resulted in groundbreaking products that changed the world.

Jobs believed deeply in the power of design and the user experience. He once said, "Design is not just what it looks like and feels like. Design is how it works." This philosophy was evident in all of Apple's products, which were known for their intuitive interfaces and sleek aesthetics.

Jobs's leadership style also included an element of showmanship. He was a master of the product launch event, often creating immense anticipation and excitement around new products. His presentations, known as "Stevenotes," were meticulously crafted to highlight the features and advantages of Apple's products, often ending with the famous line, "One more thing," before revealing a major surprise. Jobs was a strong advocate for simplicity in design. He believed that simplicity was the ultimate sophistication and often challenged his teams to eliminate unnecessary features and focus on the core user experience. For example, he famously simplified the design of the iPod by eliminating physical buttons in favor of a touch-sensitive scroll wheel. Jobs was also a proponent of the end-to-end control of hardware and software, ensuring that all aspects of Apple's products were seamlessly integrated and provided a cohesive user experience.

The Expansion of Apple's Retail Strategy

Under Jobs's leadership, Apple expanded its retail strategy to create a direct connection with consumers. The first Apple Store opened in Tysons Corner, Virginia, in 2001, and the concept quickly proved successful. Apple Stores were designed to provide an immersive and interactive experience, showcasing the company's products in a stylish and inviting environment.

The success of Apple Stores was due in part to their innovative design and exceptional customer service. The stores featured open layouts, large glass windows, and knowledgeable staff who could assist customers with any questions or issues. This approach helped build a loyal customer base and provided Apple with valuable feedback that influenced future product development.

Apple's retail strategy also included the creation of flagship stores in prominent locations around the world. These stores, often architectural masterpieces in their own right, became destinations for Apple fans and tourists alike. The Fifth Avenue store in New York City, with its iconic glass cube entrance, is one of the most famous examples, drawing millions of visitors each year.

> **Fun Fact**
>
> The store on Fifth Avenue in New York City, with its iconic glass cube entrance, is one of the most photographed landmarks in the city. The glass cube design was personally overseen by Jobs, who insisted on the highest quality materials and craftsmanship. The Fifth Avenue store is open 24/7, 365 days a year, making it a unique and accessible destination for Apple customers.

Apple store in Central Park

Major Product Launches and Their Significance

During this period, Apple launched several major products that solidified its position as a leader in technology and innovation. In addition to the iPod, iPhone, and iPad, Apple introduced the MacBook Pro, a high-performance laptop designed for professionals, and the MacBook Air, an ultra-thin and lightweight laptop that redefined portable computing.

Each of these products had a significant impact on their respective markets. The MacBook Pro became a favorite among creative professionals for its powerful performance and advanced features. The MacBook Air set new standards for portability and design, influencing the development of ultrabooks by other manufacturers.

Apple also introduced significant updates to its Mac operating system, enhancing the user experience and integrating more seamlessly with its mobile devices. Features such as the App Store for Mac, iCloud for synchronization across devices, and various software improvements helped create a cohesive ecosystem that encouraged users to stay within the Apple product family.

2010 MacBook Air

The introduction of the iPhone 4 in 2010 marked the first time Apple used a high-resolution "Retina" display, which set a new standard for screen clarity and sharpness in mobile devices. The term "Retina" was coined by Apple to describe a display with a pixel density so high that the human eye could not distinguish individual pixels at a normal viewing distance. This innovation not only enhanced the visual experience for users but also pushed competitors to improve their own display technologies.

In addition to hardware advancements, Apple continued to innovate with its software offerings. iOS, the operating system powering the iPhone and iPad, received regular updates that introduced new features and improvements. Updates like iOS 4 brought multitasking capabilities to iOS devices, while iOS 5 introduced iCloud, Apple's cloud storage service, which seamlessly synchronized content across devices. These

> **Fun Fact**
>
> The iPhone 4 sparked controversy due to reports of reception issues when the phone was held in a certain way—a phenomenon humorously referred to as "Antennagate."

updates not only enhanced the functionality of Apple's products but also reinforced the company's commitment to providing a cohesive user experience across its ecosystem. The iPhone 4 was also notable for its redesigned exterior, featuring a stainless steel frame and a glass back. This design was a departure from previous iPhone models and was intended to enhance durability and aesthetic appeal.

iPhone 4 (Black)

Building a Global Brand

Under Jobs's leadership, Apple transformed from a struggling company into a global powerhouse. Apple's brand became synonymous with innovation, quality, and design. The company's products were not only functional but also desirable, often seen as status symbols and a reflection of the user's identity.

Jobs's marketing genius played a crucial role in building Apple's brand. He understood the importance of storytelling and creating an emotional connection with consumers. Product launches were meticulously planned and executed, with Jobs often delivering keynote presentations that generated immense excitement and anticipation.

Apple's global expansion was also fueled by strategic decisions such as opening retail stores in key international markets and forming partnerships with major carriers and distributors. This approach helped Apple reach a wider audience and establish a strong presence in countries around the world.

From 2001 to 2011, Steve Jobs led Apple through a period of unparalleled innovation and growth. The launch of groundbreaking products like the iPod, iPhone, and iPad transformed not only Apple but entire industries. Jobs's visionary leadership, attention to detail, and focus on design and user experience set new standards for technology and established Apple as one of the most influential companies in the world.

During this decade, Apple built a global brand that resonated with consumers and set the stage for future successes. Jobs's legacy of innovation and excellence continues to inspire and influence the tech industry and beyond, leaving an indelible mark on the world. The impact of his work is still felt today, with Apple continuing to lead in innovation and design, building on the foundation that Jobs helped establish.

8

Personal Life

Relationships and Family

Steve Jobs had a fascinating and sometimes complicated family life. He was adopted as a baby by Paul and Clara Jobs, a loving couple who could not have children of their own. Paul was a machinist and taught Steve how to work with his hands, fostering his early interest in electronics and mechanics. Clara was an accountant, who taught Steve to read before he started school. Steve always spoke highly of his adoptive parents, saying they were his real parents.

As Steve grew older, he discovered he had a biological sister named Mona Simpson, who would later become a well-known novelist. They developed a close relationship after meeting as adults. Steve often said that finding Mona was one of the most wonderful things in his life.

In 1991, Steve married Laurene Powell. The two met when Steve was giving a lecture at Stanford University. Laurene, a business student, caught Steve's eye, and they quickly fell in love. Their wedding was a small ceremony at the Ahwahnee Hotel in Yosemite National Park. Together, they had three children: Reed,

Erin, and Eve. Steve was very private about his family life, but it was clear he loved his children deeply.

Before marrying Laurene, Steve had a daughter named Lisa Brennan-Jobs with his high school girlfriend, Chrisann Brennan. At first, Steve denied paternity, which caused tension and difficulties for Lisa and her mother. However, Steve later accepted Lisa as his daughter and she became a part of his family. In fact, one of Apple's early computers, the Lisa, was named after her.

Apple Lisa at VCFB 2019

Personal Struggles and Health Issues

Steve Jobs faced numerous personal struggles throughout his life. One of the most significant challenges was his health. In 2003, he was diagnosed with a rare form of pancreatic cancer. This type of cancer is particularly difficult to treat, and Steve chose to explore alternative treatments before opting for surgery. He tried special diets, acupuncture, and other unconventional methods in an attempt to heal himself naturally.

Despite these efforts, Steve's health continued to decline. In 2009, he underwent a liver transplant as the cancer had spread. Throughout his illness, Steve continued to work, often participating in major product launches and company decisions from his home. His determination to stay involved with Apple, even during his most challenging health battles, showed his incredible dedication to his work.

In 2011, Steve Jobs resigned as CEO of Apple, acknowledging that he could no longer meet the demands of the job. He passed away on October 5, 2011, at the age of 56. His death was a significant loss to the technology world, and he was mourned by millions of people worldwide.

Jobs's Approach to Balancing Work and Personal Life

Steve Jobs was known for his relentless work ethic and his intense focus on his projects. He often worked long hours and demanded the same dedication from his employees. This intensity sometimes made it difficult for him to balance his work and personal life. However, Steve did value his time with his family and made efforts to be present for them.

Steve and Laurene enjoyed going on long walks together, where they would talk about everything from business ideas to family matters. He also loved spending time with his children. Steve was known to take family vacations, where he could relax and disconnect from his hectic work life. One of his favorite vacation spots was Hawaii, where he could unwind and enjoy the beautiful scenery.

Despite his busy schedule, Steve made it a point to have family dinners and attend important events in his children's lives. He believed that these moments were crucial for maintaining a strong family bond. Balancing work and personal life was never easy for Steve, but he recognized the importance of being there for his loved ones.

Philanthropy and Legacy

While Steve Jobs was not as publicly philanthropic as some other tech moguls, he did contribute to various causes, particularly in the areas of education and the arts. He made significant donations to schools and educational programs, as well as to organizations supporting the arts. His wife, Laurene Powell Jobs, continues his legacy of philanthropy through the Emerson Collective, an organization she founded that focuses on social justice, education, and environmental issues.

Steve Jobs with Macintosh

Steve's legacy extends far beyond his financial contributions. He revolutionized multiple industries, including personal computing, animation, music, and telecommunications. The products he helped create, such as the Macintosh, iPod, iPhone, and iPad, have transformed the way people live and interact with technology. His innovative vision and commitment to excellence continue to inspire entrepreneurs and innovators around the world.

Lesser-Known Personal Anecdotes and Stories

There are many interesting and lesser-known stories about Steve Jobs that give a glimpse into his unique personality. For example, Steve loved to take barefoot walks in the garden. He believed that walking barefoot helped him think more clearly and stay grounded.

Steve was also known for his minimalist approach to life. He famously wore the same outfit every day: a black turtleneck, jeans, and sneakers. This uniform was not just a fashion choice but a way to simplify his life and reduce the number of decisions he had to make each day. This focus on simplicity extended to his diet as well; at various times, Steve followed strict diets, including a fruitarian diet where he ate only fruits.

Another interesting aspect of Steve's life was his deep interest in Zen Buddhism. In the 1970s, he traveled to India in search of spiritual enlightenment. This journey had a profound impact on him and influenced his design philosophy. He admired the simplicity and focus of Zen principles, which can be seen in the clean, uncluttered design of Apple products.

Influences on His Personal Philosophy

Steve Jobs was influenced by many factors throughout his life. His adoptive father, Paul Jobs, played a significant role in shaping his work ethic and attention to detail. Paul taught Steve the importance of craftsmanship and taking pride in one's work, lessons that Steve carried with him throughout his career.

His experiences with Zen Buddhism and his trip to India also had a profound impact on his personal philosophy. He learned the value of simplicity, focus, and being present in the moment. These principles guided his approach to design and product development, leading to the creation of some of the most iconic and user-friendly products in the technology industry.

Steve was also inspired by creative thinkers and artists. He admired people who pushed the boundaries of what was possible and believed in the power of combining technology with the humanities. This belief was reflected in his famous quote, "The people who are crazy enough to think they can change the world are the ones who do."

One of Steve's favorite quotes was from the poet William Blake: "Stay hungry, stay foolish." This quote encapsulated his approach to life and work. He believed in always being curious, always learning, and never being afraid to take risks. Steve lived by these words, constantly pushing the boundaries of what was possible and encouraging others to do the same.

Personal Habits and Interests

Steve Jobs had several habits and interests that shaped his personal life and contributed to his creativity. He was known for his strict dietary habits. At different times in his life, he followed a variety of diets, including veganism and fruitarianism. He believed that a clean and simple diet helped him stay focused and energized.

Steve also practiced mindfulness and meditation. His interest in Zen Buddhism led him to regularly meditate, which he found to be a valuable way to clear his mind and enhance his creativity. This practice helped him manage stress and maintain his intense work schedule.

In addition to his spiritual practices, Steve had a passion for the arts. He enjoyed music, particularly Bob Dylan and The Beatles, whose lyrics and melodies inspired him. He was also a fan of calligraphy, which he studied briefly in college. This interest in beautiful typography later influenced the design of Apple's products, making them not only functional but also aesthetically pleasing.

Friendship and Mentorship

Steve Jobs valued his friendships and often sought advice and inspiration from those he admired. One of his closest friends was Larry Ellison, the co-founder of Oracle Corporation. They shared a deep bond and often spent time together discussing business, technology, and life.

Steve also had a mentor in Robert Friedland, a charismatic and somewhat unconventional entrepreneur. Friedland introduced Steve to the ideas of Eastern spirituality and meditation, which had a lasting impact on him.

Another significant figure in Steve's life was Mike Markkula, an early investor in Apple and a mentor to Steve. Markkula provided valuable business advice and helped guide Apple during its early years. He taught Steve important lessons about marketing, business strategy, and leadership.

Fun Facts About Steve Jobs's Personal Life

- Barefoot Meetings: Steve Jobs was known to conduct business meetings while walking barefoot in his garden. He believed that being in a natural setting helped him think more creatively.
- Fruit Company: When Steve started Apple, he was a strict fruitarian and even considered naming the company "Apple" because it sounded fun, spirited, and not intimidating.
- Calligraphy Classes: After dropping out of Reed College, Steve Jobs continued to sit in on a calligraphy class. He later credited this class with teaching him about typefaces and design, which influenced the typography used in Apple products.
- Love for Bob Dylan: Steve was a huge Bob Dylan fan. He often quoted Dylan lyrics and had a vast collection of Dylan memorabilia. He even used a Dylan song, "The Times They Are A-Changin," in an early Apple commercial.
- Enchanted by India: Steve's trip to India in search of spiritual enlightenment left a lasting impression on him. He came back with a shaved head and wearing traditional Indian clothing, embracing a minimalist lifestyle that influenced his approach to product design.

9

Final Years and Legacy (2011-Present)

Jobs's Resignation and Tim Cook's Succession

In August 2011, Steve Jobs made the difficult decision to step down as CEO of Apple due to his deteriorating health. He recommended Tim Cook, then the Chief Operating Officer, as his successor. Steve had long recognized Tim's abilities and trusted him implicitly to carry forward Apple's vision. Tim Cook had been managing Apple's day-to-day operations during Steve's medical leaves, proving his capability as a leader.

Tim Cook's tenure began amidst concerns about whether anyone could fill Steve's shoes. However, Tim quickly demonstrated his leadership by focusing on Apple's core strengths while also expanding into new areas. Under his guidance, Apple introduced groundbreaking products like the Apple Watch and services like Apple Music and Apple Pay. Tim maintained Steve's emphasis on innovation and quality, ensuring that Apple stayed at the forefront of the tech industry.

Jobs's Passing and the Global Reaction

Steve Jobs passed away on October 5, 2011, at the age of 56, after a long battle with pancreatic cancer. The news of his passing was a moment of global mourning. Tributes poured in from around the world, reflecting the profound impact Steve had on technology and culture. Apple's website displayed a simple, heartfelt message: "Apple has lost a visionary and creative genius, and the world has lost an amazing human being."

Tim Cook

Public memorials sprang up at Apple stores worldwide, where fans left flowers, messages, and tributes. Prominent figures, including political leaders, business rivals, and celebrities, shared their condolences and memories. President Barack Obama called Steve "among the greatest of American innovators," and Bill Gates remarked that "the world rarely sees someone who has had the profound impact Steve has had."

Fun Fact

Tim Cook was known for his discipline and routine, reportedly starting his day at 4:30 AM to send emails and then hitting the gym.

Long-Term Impact on Apple and Technology

After Steve Jobs's passing in 2011, Apple has continued to flourish under the leadership of Tim Cook. Steve's emphasis on innovation and excellence laid a strong foundation for

> **Fun Fact**
> On the day of his passing, the lights of the iconic Apple logo at the company's retail stores were dimmed in tribute to Steve Jobs.

the company, allowing it to thrive even in his absence. Apple has introduced several new products and technologies that have further cemented its position as a leader in the tech industry.

One of the most significant new products is the Apple Watch, introduced in 2015. The Apple Watch quickly became the best-selling wearable device, integrating health and fitness tracking with notifications and other smart features. This product expanded Apple's ecosystem, demonstrating the company's ability to innovate in new categories.

Apple has also made significant strides in services, an area Steve Jobs had begun to explore but which has grown exponentially under Tim Cook. Services like Apple Music, Apple TV+, Apple Arcade, and iCloud have become major revenue sources for the company. This diversification has helped Apple maintain robust financial health and continue to grow.

Apple Watch, 2015

Advances in Hardware and Software

> **Fun Fact**
> The Apple Watch can detect irregular heart rhythms and has been credited with saving lives by alerting users to potential heart issues.

Apple has consistently pushed the boundaries of hardware and software design. The introduction of the M1 chip in 2020 marked a significant milestone. This custom-designed chip for Macs provided remarkable improvements in performance and energy efficiency, underscoring Apple's commitment to controlling every aspect of its products. The M1 chip has been followed by even more powerful iterations like the M1 Pro, M1 Max, and M2 chips, setting new benchmarks in the industry.

On the software front, Apple has continued to refine its operating systems, including iOS, macOS, watchOS, and tvOS. These systems are known for their seamless integration, user-friendly interfaces, and robust security features. Regular updates ensure that users have access to the latest features and improvements, keeping Apple devices at the forefront of technology. Apple's macOS Catalina introduced Sidecar, a feature that allows users to use their iPad as a second display for their Mac, showcasing Apple's seamless ecosystem integration.

Impact on Design and User Experience

Steve Jobs's legacy of prioritizing design and user experience is evident in Apple's products today. The minimalist aesthetic and intuitive interfaces that Steve championed continue to define Apple's design philosophy. Products like the iPhone, iPad, and MacBook remain benchmarks in industrial design, often imitated by competitors but rarely matched in quality and user satisfaction.

Apple's approach to design extends beyond hardware to retail spaces. The Apple Store experience, with its clean lines, open spaces, and knowledgeable staff, reflects Steve's vision of a seamless and engaging user experience. These stores have become iconic, often serving as community hubs where people can learn about and interact with technology. The first Apple Store opened in Tysons Corner, Virginia, in 2001. Today, there are over 500 Apple Stores worldwide, attracting millions of visitors each year.

Influence on Industry Standards and Competitors

Steve Jobs's influence has also shaped broader industry standards. His insistence on high-quality materials and precise manufacturing processes raised the bar for consumer electronics. This focus on premium quality has forced competitors to elevate their own products to remain competitive. Features like high-resolution displays, advanced cameras, and efficient operating systems that are now industry standards were pioneered by Apple.

The App Store, introduced by Apple in 2008, revolutionized how software is distributed and monetized. It created a new economy for app developers and set a precedent for digital marketplaces. The success of the App Store prompted other tech giants like Google and Microsoft to develop their own app ecosystems, fundamentally changing the software industry. The App Store reached 10,000 apps in just six months after its launch in 2008. As of now, it offers over 2 million apps to users worldwide.

Environmental Initiatives and Corporate Responsibility

Apple has also become a leader in environmental sustainability, a focus that began under Steve Jobs and has been expanded by Tim Cook. The company has committed to using 100% recycled or renewable materials in its products. Initiatives like the Daisy robot, which disassembles iPhones to recover valuable materials, demonstrate Apple's commitment to reducing its environmental impact.

Apple's headquarters, Apple Park, reflects these values with its eco-friendly design. The campus is powered by 100% renewable energy and features extensive green spaces. Apple's commitment to sustainability has influenced other tech companies to adopt greener practices, showcasing the company's role as a leader in corporate responsibility.

Apple Park

Financial Growth and Market Influence

Since Steve Jobs's return to Apple in 1997, the company's financial growth has been astonishing. From near bankruptcy, Apple became the first U.S. company to reach a market valuation of $1 trillion in 2018. This growth has continued, with Apple hitting a $2 trillion valuation just two years later in 2020, and nearing $3 trillion in 2023. This financial success has provided Apple with the resources to invest heavily in research and development, ensuring its continued leadership in innovation.

Apple's influence extends to stock markets and the global economy. The company's performance is often seen as a bellwether for the tech industry and the broader market. Apple's success has spurred the growth of an entire ecosystem

> **Fun Fact**
>
> If you had bought $1,000 worth of Apple stock when Steve Jobs returned to the company in 1997, your investment would be worth over $400,000 today.

of suppliers, developers, and accessories manufacturers, further magnifying its economic impact.

Educational and Cultural Impact

Steve Jobs's belief in the power of technology to transform education continues to influence Apple's initiatives in this sector. Programs like Apple Distinguished Schools and Everyone Can Code provide educational institutions with the tools and curriculum to foster creativity and technical skills in students. The iPad has become a valuable educational tool, used in classrooms around the world to enhance learning experiences.

Statue of Steve Jobs in Budapest

Culturally, Steve Jobs's story and philosophy have become a source of inspiration. His famous commencement speech at Stanford University in 2005, where he urged graduates to "stay hungry, stay foolish," is frequently cited for its motivational wisdom. Steve's approach to life and work, emphasizing passion, perseverance, and creativity, continues to resonate with people across generations.

> **Fun Fact**
> Steve Jobs was a fan of calligraphy, and his appreciation for beautiful fonts influenced the typeface choices in the original Macintosh, making it the first computer to offer multiple typefaces.

Cultural and Entrepreneurial Legacy

Redefining Innovation and Design

Steve Jobs fundamentally changed how the world views innovation and design. He believed that technology should not only be functional but also beautiful and easy to use. This philosophy was evident in every Apple product, from the sleek lines of the MacBook to the intuitive interface of the iPhone. Jobs's insistence on simplicity and elegance set new standards for product design across industries.

Apple's products have become cultural icons, symbolizing cutting-edge technology and sophisticated design. The iPhone, in particular, revolutionized the smartphone industry and influenced the design of countless other products. Jobs's approach to design has inspired designers and engineers to prioritize aesthetics and user experience, leading to a broader cultural appreciation for well-designed technology.

Transforming Consumer Behavior

Steve Jobs's vision extended beyond product design to transforming how people interact with technology. The introduction of the iTunes Store revolutionized the music industry by providing a legal and convenient way to purchase and download music. This shift not only helped combat piracy but also changed how people consumed media.

The App Store, launched in 2008, created a new economy for app developers and changed the way people use their phones. It made smartphones more versatile by providing access to a vast array of applications, from games to productivity tools. This innovation has influenced how other digital marketplaces operate and continues to shape consumer behavior in the digital age. The App Store reached one million apps in 2013, just five years after its launch, highlighting its massive influence on the software industry.

Inspirational Leadership and Vision

Steve Jobs is often celebrated for his unique leadership style and visionary thinking. His ability to foresee trends and drive innovation made him a role model for entrepreneurs and business leaders worldwide. Jobs's famous motto, "Stay hungry, stay foolish," from his 2005 Stanford University commencement speech, encourages individuals to pursue their passions relentlessly and embrace unconventional thinking.

Jobs's leadership was characterized by his ability to push his teams to achieve the impossible. He had a knack for identifying and nurturing talent, and he inspired those around him to strive for excellence. His story of resilience, from being ousted from Apple to founding NeXT and then returning to lead Apple to unprecedented success, is a powerful narrative of perseverance and visionary leadership.

Impact on Entrepreneurship

> **Fun Fact**
> Steve Jobs's favorite fruit was apples, which influenced the naming of the company he co-founded. The apple in the logo originally had a bite taken out of it to avoid confusion with a cherry.

Steve Jobs's entrepreneurial legacy is marked by his commitment to innovation, risk-taking, and an unwavering focus on the customer. He co-founded Apple in his parents' garage, and under his leadership, the company grew into one of the most valuable and influential corporations in the world. Jobs's story has inspired countless entrepreneurs to start their ventures, believing that with vision and determination, they too can create something world-changing.

Jobs demonstrated that successful entrepreneurship requires not only a great idea but also the ability to execute that idea effectively. His attention to detail, from product development to marketing, set a high standard for startups and established businesses alike. Entrepreneurs continue to look up to Jobs as a model for how to combine creativity, business acumen, and a relentless pursuit of excellence.

Shaping Corporate Culture

Steve Jobs's approach to corporate culture has left a lasting impact on how companies are structured and operate. At Apple, Jobs fostered a culture of innovation, secrecy, and excellence. He believed in small, focused teams that could work collaboratively to achieve great things. This emphasis on teamwork and creativity helped Apple maintain its competitive edge and produce groundbreaking products.

Jobs also valued the intersection of technology and the humanities, promoting a culture that embraced both engineering and artistic perspectives. This holistic approach to problem-solving and innovation has influenced many other companies, encouraging them to value diverse skills and viewpoints within their teams.

> **Fun Fact**
> Steve Jobs was known for his signature black turtleneck, jeans, and New Balance sneakers, a look he adopted after being inspired by the uniformity and simplicity of Japanese work culture.

Influence on Education and Creativity

Steve Jobs believed deeply in the power of education and creativity. He often spoke about the importance of following one's passions and pursuing lifelong learning. Under his leadership, Apple developed educational initiatives and tools aimed at fostering creativity and innovation in students. Products like the iPad have become integral to modern classrooms, enhancing learning experiences and providing students with new ways to engage with information.

> **Fun Fact**
>
> Steve Jobs's appreciation for calligraphy, which he studied in college, influenced the typography and design aesthetics of the Macintosh computer, making it the first computer to offer multiple typefaces and proportionally spaced fonts.

Jobs's influence extends to the arts as well. He saw technology as a tool to empower creative expression, and his work at Apple and Pixar reflects this belief. By bridging the gap between technology and the arts, Jobs has inspired a generation of creatives to explore new mediums and push the boundaries of their work.

Posthumous Honors and Recognitions

After his passing, Steve Jobs received numerous honors and recognitions. He was posthumously awarded the Grammy Trustees Award for his contributions to the music industry through iTunes and the iPod. In 2012, he was inducted into the California Hall of Fame. Time Magazine included him in its list of the 20 most influential Americans of all time.

In 2013, Ashton Kutcher portrayed Steve Jobs in the biographical film "Jobs," and in 2015, Michael Fassbender starred in "Steve Jobs," a film directed by Danny Boyle and written by Aaron Sorkin. Both films highlighted different aspects of Steve's life and work, bringing his story to a wider audience. These portrayals helped keep his legacy alive, demonstrating his impact on popular culture.

In 2017, the Steve Jobs Theaterwas opened on Apple's new campus, Apple Park. This stunning auditorium is a tribute to Steve's legacy and a venue for future Apple product launches and events. The theater stands as a testament to his vision and dedication to excellence, designed with the same meticulous attention to detail that characterized his work.

Reflections from Family, Friends, and Colleagues

Many people who knew Steve Jobs have shared their reflections and memories, painting a picture of a complex and driven individual. His wife, Laurene Powell Jobs, spoke of his deep love for his family and his passion for creating products that could change the world. She continues to honor his legacy through her philanthropic work, particularly in education and social justice.

Medal of Freedom awarded to Steve Jobs (received by his widow Laurene Powell Jobs)

Steve's children have described him as a loving father who always encouraged them to pursue their passions. His friends and colleagues, like Tim Cook and Jony Ive, have shared stories about his intense focus and his ability to inspire those around him to achieve greatness. Bill Gates, Steve's longtime friend and rival, called him "profoundly inspiring" and admired his ability to "think differently."

> **Fun Fact**
>
> Steve Jobs and Bill Gates had a famously competitive relationship, but they also had deep respect for each other. They once joked about their rivalry during a joint interview at a tech conference in 2007.

Ongoing Influence on Future Generations

Steve Jobs's influence continues to inspire future generations of innovators and entrepreneurs. His story is taught in business schools around the world, and his approach to design and product development remains a model for companies everywhere. Steve's belief in the power of combining technology with the arts has led to new innovations and creative solutions in various fields.

Young entrepreneurs look up to Steve as an example of how to pursue their dreams relentlessly. His famous motto, "Stay hungry, stay foolish," encourages people to keep pushing boundaries and never settle for the status quo. Steve Jobs's legacy is not just in the products he created but in the mindset he fostered—a mindset of curiosity, creativity, and boldness.

> **Fun Fact**
> Steve Jobs was a fan of Bob Dylan and often drew inspiration from his lyrics. He even named a Macintosh computer after a Dylan song, "The Freewheelin' Bob Dylan."

Steve Jobs's final years were marked by significant challenges and incredible achievements. His resignation and passing were deeply felt by the world, but his legacy continues to thrive. From his long-term impact on Apple and technology to his cultural and entrepreneurial influence, Steve Jobs remains a beacon of innovation and inspiration. His posthumous honors and the reflections of those who knew him best serve as a testament to his extraordinary life and enduring impact. As future generations continue to be inspired by his story, Steve Jobs's legacy will undoubtedly continue to shape the world for years to come.

10

Lessons From Steve Jobs's Life

Key Takeaways for Aspiring Innovators and Entrepreneurs

Think Differently: One of Steve Jobs's most enduring lessons is the importance of thinking differently. Jobs believed in challenging the status quo and finding innovative solutions to problems. He encouraged others to break free from conventional thinking and explore new possibilities. This mindset led to groundbreaking products like the iPhone, which revolutionized the mobile phone industry.

Focus on Quality: Jobs was known for his obsessive attention to detail and commitment to quality. He believed that every aspect of a product, from its design to its user experience, should be meticulously crafted. This focus on excellence ensured that Apple products stood out in the market and garnered a loyal customer base. For aspiring entrepreneurs, this means that investing time and resources in perfecting their products can lead to long-term success.

Embrace Failure: Throughout his career, Jobs faced numerous setbacks, including being ousted from Apple in 1985. Instead of giving up, he used these experiences to learn and grow. His time away from Apple led to the creation of NeXT and the revitalization of Pixar, both of which played crucial roles in his eventual return to Apple. Jobs's ability to bounce back from failure teaches aspiring entrepreneurs the value of resilience and learning from mistakes.

> **Fun Fact**
> Steve Jobs once said, "The only way to do great work is to love what you do." This quote has become a mantra for many entrepreneurs and creatives.

Pursue Your Passion: Jobs often spoke about the importance of following one's passions. He believed that passion was a critical driver of success because it fuels perseverance and creativity. His own passion for technology and design propelled him to create products that have changed the world. For aspiring innovators, pursuing what they love can lead to both personal fulfillment and professional success.

Lessons on Leadership and Management

Inspire and Motivate: Steve Jobs was known for his ability to inspire and motivate his team. He had a clear vision for Apple and was able to communicate it compellingly. Jobs's passion and charisma energized his employees, driving them to achieve extraordinary results. Effective leadership involves inspiring others to share in a vision and motivating them to strive for excellence.

Foster Innovation: Jobs created an environment at Apple that fostered innovation. He encouraged his team to think creatively and take risks. By promoting a culture of experimentation and curiosity, Jobs ensured that Apple remained at the forefront of technological advancements. Leaders can learn from this by creating a workplace where new ideas are welcomed and innovation is a core value.

Build Strong Teams: Jobs recognized the importance of surrounding himself with talented individuals. He was adept at identifying and recruiting top talent, and he trusted his team to execute his vision. Strong leaders understand the value of building and nurturing teams of skilled and dedicated people who can collaborate effectively.

The Importance of Resilience and Perseverance

Overcoming Adversity: Steve Jobs's life was marked by significant challenges and setbacks. From being adopted as a child to being fired from Apple, Jobs faced adversity with determination. His story is a testament to the power of resilience and the ability to turn obstacles into opportunities. Aspiring innovators can learn that setbacks are not the end but can be catalysts for growth and reinvention.

Persistence Pays Off: Jobs's journey illustrates that persistence is crucial for achieving long-term success. His relentless pursuit of his goals, even in the face of failure, ultimately led to some of the most significant achievements in the tech industry. Entrepreneurs should remember that persistence, combined with a clear vision and hard work, can lead to remarkable outcomes.

President Ronald Reagan presents the 1985 National Technology Awards to Steven Jobs

Balancing Ambition with Humility

Stay Grounded: Despite his success, Steve Jobs valued humility. He understood the importance of staying grounded and not letting success go to his head. Jobs maintained a focus on continuous improvement and remained open to new ideas and feedback. Balancing ambition with humility ensures that leaders stay connected to their goals and continue to strive for excellence without becoming complacent.

Value Contributions: Jobs recognized the contributions of others and valued collaboration. While he was a visionary, he understood that achieving his vision required the efforts of a talented team. Acknowledging and appreciating the work of others fosters a positive work environment and encourages collective success.

Focus on the Bigger Picture: Jobs's ambition was always tempered by a focus on the bigger picture. He was driven by a desire to make a meaningful impact on the world, not just by personal gain. This broader perspective allowed him to make decisions that aligned with his long-term vision and values. Balancing ambition with a sense of purpose can lead to more sustainable and impactful success.

Conclusion

Newton Apple 1976

Rainbow Apple 1977

Simplified Apple 1998 onwards

Timeline of Major Events in Steve Jobs's Life

- 1955: Born on February 24 in San Francisco, California.
- 1976: Jobs and Steve Wozniak found Apple Computer, Inc. in the Jobs family garage.
- 1984: Apple launches the Macintosh, the first mass-market personal computer with a graphical user interface.
- 1985: Jobs resigns from Apple after a power struggle with the board of directors.
- 1986: Jobs founds NeXT Inc., a computer platform development company.
- 1996: Apple acquires NeXT, bringing Steve Jobs back to the company.
- 1997: Jobs becomes the interim CEO of Apple.
- 1998: Apple introduces the iMac, signaling the beginning of a new era of design and innovation.
- 2001: Apple launches the iPod, revolutionizing the music industry.
- 2007: The iPhone is introduced, transforming the smartphone market.
- 2010: Apple introduces the iPad, creating a new category of tablet devices.
- 2011: Steve Jobs passes away on October 5, at the age of 56.

List of Major Products and Innovations

- Apple I (1976)
- Apple II (1977)
- Macintosh (1984)
- NeXT Computer (1988)
- iMac (1998)
- iPod (2001)
- iTunes Store (2003)
- iPhone (2007)
- App Store (2008)
- iPad (2010)
- MacBook Air (2008)
- Apple Watch (2015)